DON'T KNOW MUCH ABOUT®

THE
PILGRIMS

KENNETH C. DAVIS
ILLUSTRATED BY S. D. SCHINDLER

HarperCollins*Publishers*

Acknowledgments

An author's name goes on the cover of a book. But behind that book are a great many people who make it all happen. I would like to thank all of the wonderful people at HarperCollins who helped make this book a reality, including Susan Katz, Kate Morgan Jackson, Barbara Lalicki, Harriett Barton, Rosemary Brosnan, Meredith Charpentier, Anne Dunn, Dana Hayward, Maggie Herold, Fumi Kosaka, Marisa Miller, Rachel Orr, and Katherine Rogers. I would also like to thank David Black, Joy Tutela, and Alix Reid for their friendship, assistance, and great ideas. My wife, Joann, and my children, Jenny and Colin, are always a source of inspiration, joy, and support. Without them, I could not do my work.

I especially thank April Prince for her devoted efforts and unique contributions. This book would not have been possible without her tireless work, imagination, and creativity.

The illustrator gratefully acknowledges Plimoth Plantation for their book *Mayflower II,* published by Fort Church Publishers, Inc., Little Compton, RI, 1993, which he used as a reference for the following illustrations: end papers, p. 11—man with map, p. 14—man cooking, p. 18—map.

Library of Congress Cataloging-in-Publication Data
Davis, Kenneth C.
   Don't know much about the Pilgrims / by Kenneth C. Davis ; illustrated by S. D. Schindler.
        p.   cm.
   Summary: Questions and answers present information about who the pilgrims were, how and why they came to America on the Mayflower, and what happened in the colony of New Plymouth.
   ISBN 0-06-028609-1 — ISBN 0-06-028610-5 (lib. bdg.)
   1. Pilgrims (New Plymouth Colony)—Juvenile literature.
2. Mayflower (Ship)—Juvenile literature.   3. Massachusetts—History—New Plymouth, 1620–1691—Juvenile literature.
[1. Pilgrims (New Plymouth Colony)—Miscellanea.   2. Mayflower (Ship)—Miscellanea.   3. Massachusetts—History—New Plymouth, 1620–1691—Miscellanea.   4. Questions and answers.]
I. Schindler, S. D., ill.   II. Title.
F68 .D27   2002   00-23535
974.48'202—dc21

Design by Charles Yuen
1   2   3   4   5   6   7   8   9   10
❖
First Edition

✍ INTRODUCTION ✍

What's your favorite part of Thanksgiving dinner? The turkey? The stuffing and mashed potatoes? If you're like me, the answer is easy. It's the cranberries and pumpkin pie! Well, guess what? When the Pilgrims sat down to enjoy their big harvest dinner in America about four hundred years ago, they didn't eat many of the things we like to eat today. The holiday menu we love is just one of the many wrong ideas that some Americans have about Thanksgiving Day and the people we celebrate each November, the Pilgrims of Plymouth Plantation.

Every year in the fall, schools and stores are decorated with cardboard cutouts of Pilgrims dressed in clunky shoes and funny black hats. And that is about all some people know about this group of English men, women, and children who sailed to America long ago, in search of a better life. But the real story of who these people were, what they looked like, why they came to America, and how they lived is told in DON'T KNOW MUCH ABOUT® THE PILGRIMS. This is a true tale of the hard days of hunger, cold, and danger. It's an incredible story about real people, especially children, who struggled to survive in the early days of America, and about the Native Americans who helped them. When you have finished reading the book and know what life was like for a Pilgrim child four hundred years ago, you will have a real reason to be thankful—you'll be glad that you weren't around back then!

You know they wore tall black hats and ate turkey and cranberries. But who were the Pilgrims, really?

The early settlers who sailed on the *Mayflower* in 1620 didn't come all the way across the ocean just to see the sights. Most of them were part of a religious group of English men and women called *Puritans*. In the Puritans' day, all English people had to belong to the Church of England—and none other. The Puritans disagreed with some of the Church's ideas, especially all its fancy ceremonies and decorations. They wanted to *purify* the Church, or make it clean. (Get it—*Pur*-itan?)

Pilgrims were a special kind of Puritan. They didn't just want to purify the Church of England; they wanted to break away from it altogether. This made King James angry. The king said the Pilgrims had to shape up or ship out!

So that's just what the Pilgrims did. They made a pilgrimage to the New World, where they could worship as they pleased.

One child was born aboard the *Mayflower* during the Pilgrims' voyage. His parents named him ... Oceanus!

Did the Pilgrims call themselves Pilgrims?

Nope. The Pilgrims actually called themselves "First Comers," or "Saints." The name Pilgrim comes from a book that one of the Pilgrims, William Bradford, wrote many years after the *Mayflower* landed. He referred to his fellow settlers as "pilgrims" because a pilgrim is someone who takes a *pilgrimage*—a long journey to a holy land.

TRUE ·or· FALSE All the people aboard the *Mayflower* were Pilgrims.

False. Of the 102 passengers on board the *Mayflower*, including 34 children, only 50 passengers were Pilgrims. Even though not everyone aboard the *Mayflower* was a religious pilgrim, the whole group of settlers has become known as Pilgrims.

Who else sailed aboard the *Mayflower*?

There were:

- 25–30 sailors
- 2 dogs
- lots of rats, mice, lice, and maggots (a kind of worm that lives on rotting food)

And probably:

- cats (to chase the mice!)
- goats, pigs, and chickens

English, French, and Portuguese sailors had been fishing the waters off the New England coast for more than a hundred years before the Pilgrims landed there. Sailors returned with stories not only of the Indians but of scaly sea serpents that could swallow a whole ship in one bite. Only the bravest (or maybe the dumbest?) sailors crossed the Atlantic to the New World.

Why did the Pilgrims sail all the way to the New World?

Wouldn't it have been easier for the Pilgrims to find someplace closer to home where they could worship freely? In fact, at first they did just that.

Before the Pilgrims sailed to America, they went to Holland. That was the only country in all of Europe where people could worship any way they chose. The Pilgrims stayed in Holland from 1609 to 1620.

Even though they could worship the way they wanted to in Holland, the Pilgrims weren't very happy there. They had to work harder than they had worked in England. And parents didn't like the way their children were forgetting their English language and traditions.

To make matters worse, Holland was about to go to war with Spain. The Pilgrims decided they'd risk fighting Indians in America rather than battling the Spanish in Holland. So off to the New World it was!

Try out these Dutch words the Pilgrims learned in Holland:

Goede morgen
(HOO-de MOR-fen)
Good morning

Goede dag
(HOO-de da)
Good-bye

Danke U wel
(DONK oo vill)
Thank you very much

Did all the Pilgrims leave Holland for the New World?

No. Actually, more stayed than left. Those who did leave believed that God was calling them to go to the New World and spread His word.

NEW WORLD EXPLORATIONS BEFORE THE PILGRIMS:

c.1000   Norse captain Leif Eriksson explored Newfoundland and settled Vinland, the first European colony in North America.

1492   Christopher Columbus sailed the ocean blue (and landed in the Bahamas).

1497   John Cabot landed at Nova Scotia.

1534   Jacques Cartier sailed to Canada.

1540   Francisco de Coronado explored New Mexico and the American Southwest.

1565   St. Augustine, Florida, was settled by Spaniards.

1585   The colony of Roanoke Island, off the coast of North Carolina, was settled by the English.

1607   Jamestown, Virginia, the first permanent English settlement in the New World, was founded.

1608   Quebec City was founded.

1610   Henry Hudson explored Hudson Bay.

1614   John Smith of the Jamestown settlement explored the New England coast.

William Bradford recorded some of the Pilgrims' experiences. Describing the scene of the Pilgrims leaving Holland, he wrote, "Truly doleful was the sight of that sad and mournful parting . . . what tears did gush from every eye."

It wasn't just people that made the *Mayflower* crowded. The ship's lower decks were stacked floor to ceiling with tables, beds, rugs, chairs, chests of clothes and linens, pillows, seeds for planting, tools, dishes, food, and keepsakes. The men also brought armor, guns, and gunpowder to fight the Indians.

The sailors and the Pilgrims didn't get along very well, mostly because they were so different from one another. The Pilgrims said prayer after prayer. The sailors said anything *but* prayers.

What was life like on the *Mayflower*?

The *Mayflower* was no cruise ship. Life aboard her was:

CROWDED. No one knows exactly how big the *Mayflower* was, but we do know that it was never meant to carry so many passengers. (Do you remember how many? A whopping 102!) There was hardly any room to move, and very little privacy on board.

LOUD. All day and all night, you'd hear goats bleating, pigs oinking, chickens squawking, beams creaking, sailors and passengers shouting, wind blowing, canvas flapping, and waves crashing.

SMELLY! And guess what smelled the worst. No, not the pigs . . . the people! No one changed clothes or bathed during the sixty-six days of the trip. (Can you imagine what your friends would say if you wore the same clothes and didn't take a shower for more than two months?) Men clipped their beards and women kept their hair under caps to stay neat, but there was just no way to stay clean. And the bathroom situation was . . . interesting. Everyone used buckets, which they emptied overboard.

ITCHY. Lice and fleas camped out in everyone's clothes and hair.

COLD AND WET. Brrrr! The icy winter wind and rain came right through the cracks in the *Mayflower*'s deck and fell onto the passengers. Since there was no heat on board, there was no way to dry off until the sun came out.

If April showers bring May flowers, what do May flowers bring?

Pilgrims!

DARK AND CRAMPED. There was very little light below deck. And the five-foot-high ceilings were not tall enough for most adults to stand up straight.

BUMPY. The water was rough, the winds wicked. The rocking and rolling of the ship made almost everyone seasick. (Those buckets probably came in pretty handy, huh?)

You know the Pilgrims came to the New World for religious reasons. Can you guess what they did before each meal?

They prayed.

Today's specials aboard the *Mayflower:*

pease porridge: a thick soup of dried peas and maybe some salty beef

loblolly: hot oatmeal

poor john: salted and dried fish

stewed prunes: dried plums simmered in water to soften

What did the children on board the *Mayflower* do all day?

Much of the time the children stayed below deck out of the sailors' way. They played quiet word games or listened to the women tell stories. There were grown-up books on board, including the Bible. (Books written especially for children weren't around yet.) And every day Pilgrim children and adults sang psalms, or religious songs.

Care for some moldy cheese and stale ship's biscuits?

The menu on the *Mayflower* included these yummy items, plus dried beans and peas, salted meat, turnips, cabbages, parsnips, and onions. If you weren't too seasick to eat, you'd dine on the same old things day after day after day.

Were there hot meals on the *Mayflower*?

The Pilgrims did cook aboard the *Mayflower*, but probably not very often. The sea had to be very calm before it was safe to light a fire, because one spark could set the whole ship ablaze.

What did the Pilgrims think the New World would be like?

None of the Pilgrims knew for sure.

Imagine your parents telling you that your family is moving. You have to leave your home, friends, and school behind. You'll probably never see them again. Your mother and father don't know much about where you're going, only that it's very far away and few Americans have ever been there. They do know that there will be no friends, houses, or stores there when you arrive. Just wilderness. You might freeze or starve. Indians might kill you. But you have to be a good Pilgrim child and obey your parents. . . . And you thought taking out the garbage was bad!

The Pilgrims risked everything for their religion and ideas. They must have *really* believed in God's plan for them.

As the saying goes, if the shoe fits . . . bring 126 pairs? Since no one knew what kinds of materials the Pilgrims would find in the New World, one man, William Mullins, thought it was better to be safe than sorry. He brought 126 pairs of shoes and 13 pairs of boots to sell to his fellow settlers in America! Wonder if he thought to bring that many pairs of stockings?

After more than two months on a boat, the Pilgrims had to learn how to walk on land all over again. It probably felt a little like it does when you first get off an escalator—like the ground is still moving.

The men who went exploring wore armor and carried weapons. They were led by Captain Myles Standish, the only soldier in the group.

TRUE or FALSE Plymouth was the first place the Pilgrims landed.

False. Plymouth was the place the Pilgrims finally settled, but not the first place they landed. They did a lot of exploring before they chose Plymouth as their home.

The first place the Pilgrims landed after sixty-six days at sea was Cape Cod, a narrow, curving strip of land sticking out from what would later become the state of Massachusetts. They'd been headed for the Hudson River, which was then part of the Virginia Colony, but they'd been blown off course.

Did the passengers have a wild party to celebrate their landing?

No. But they did pray. Then they wrote a contract. Those festive Pilgrims.

When the Pilgrims finally saw land, they fell to their knees in prayers of thanks.

But soon the passengers started arguing. Now that they were in the New World, some wanted to go off on their own. But the Pilgrim leaders knew that that would be dangerous. The settlers had to stay together and help one another if they were going to survive in this strange new land. Their little group was small enough as it was. What if the Indians attacked?

To stop the fighting before anyone set foot on land, the Pilgrim leaders wrote a document now called the Mayflower Compact. The compact said that the settlers agreed to elect officers and to make laws that would serve and protect the whole group. At first some

people grumbled, but finally all forty-one adult men signed the document. Those men elected John Carver the first governor of the colony. (Women didn't get to vote.) This was the first time any British colonists had chosen their own leader.

What were the first things the Pilgrims did when their feet finally touched land again?

1) The women washed the clothes.

2) Some men stood guard while the women did the wash.

3) Others put together the *shallop*, the small craft used to explore the coast, and the rest looked around the land for a place to settle.

4) The children ran along the beaches until they couldn't run anymore. They had sixty-six days' worth of energy to use up!

Meanwhile, back on the *Mayflower*, young Francis Billington was up to no good. While his father was away exploring, Francis made some *squibs*, or simple firecrackers, and set them off inside the ship. Then he fired a musket. With all the open barrels of gunpowder nearby, it's a miracle he wasn't hurt and that the whole ship didn't go up in flames.

Did our Pilgrim forefathers ever steal?

They sure did. When the Pilgrim men were exploring the woods on Cape Cod, they found baskets of Indian corn buried in the sand. The Pilgrims had never seen corn before, but they knew it was a "goodly sight." It was like finding pots of gold!

The Pilgrims knew the corn wasn't theirs to take, but they also knew that if they didn't have enough grain to plant in the spring, they would starve. What if the wheat and rye they had brought from England wouldn't grow in the New World soil? The Pilgrims stuffed as much corn as they could into their pockets and filled a big iron kettle as well. They said they would repay the Indians later, which they did.

How did the Pilgrims know where they were going? They certainly didn't stop at a gas station to ask for directions. They had a map. Captain John Smith had explored the New England coast in 1614 and made a map for England's Prince Charles. Smith asked the prince to give the places on the map English names, which is how Plymouth got its name.

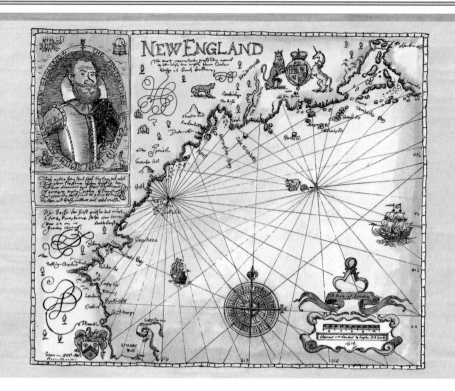

Why did the Pilgrims leave Cape Cod?

After more than a month of exploring the Cape, the Pilgrims still had not found a good place to settle. There were too many Indians and not enough fresh water. The Pilgrims began to worry—it was getting colder and colder. So eighteen of the strongest men took the shallop for one last exploring trip. Those poor men! Their clothes froze solid in the icy wind and waves.

What did the explorers find on the mainland?

The men in the shallop were blown to a place called Plymouth on their map. Plymouth wasn't perfect, but it had lots of things the Pilgrims needed.

Match each thing the Pilgrims found at
Plymouth with the reason it was important:

1. A hill

2. Freshwater springs

3. Flax and hemp

4. Wild grapes, herbs,
   onions, berries,
   fish, lobsters, crabs,
   and mussels

5. A good harbor

6. Fields that had been
   cleared by Indians
   (who were no longer
   around)

A. Drinking water

B. Ships could come and go
   with supplies.

C. Good things to eat

D. The Pilgrims could build
   their houses without the
   hard work of clearing the
   area of its tall trees.

E. The Pilgrims could make
   rope.

F. A good lookout point for
   defending the colony

Answers: 1 - F, 2 - A, 3 - E, 4 - C, 5 - B, 6 - D

Did the Pilgrims step on Plymouth Rock?

No one really knows. Legend has it that the Pilgrims
first stepped ashore at their new home atop a granite
boulder now called Plymouth Rock. It's possible, but it's
more likely that they merely landed somewhere near it.

So how did the rock get so famous? Plymouth Rock was
first mentioned 121 years after the Pilgrims landed
at Plymouth. A wharf was going to be built
where the boulder stood. Elder Thomas
Faunce, whose father had known some
of the First Comers, said that the
Pilgrims had landed on that rock. No
one could agree whether that was true,
but over the years Plymouth Rock has been
honored, moved, broken, moved again, and
honored some more.

Since the Pilgrims were building a town they would live in for the rest of their lives, they wanted to plan their village before they started building. Pretty smart, those Pilgrims. They decided to put their houses along one main street that would run alongside the town brook. The main street was really the only street in the colony. So it was simply called the Street!

Who would get the first house?

There wouldn't be time to build separate houses for everyone before winter came. Single people would move in with families, and smaller families would move in with larger ones. But before any family got a home, the Pilgrims built the Common House. The men slept there while they built the other houses. Women and children slept on the *Mayflower*. Once all the houses were completed, the Common House was used for storing tools and grain. It would be used as a church meeting house and a hospital before the first ten houses were finished.

20

It was almost Christmas. Had the Pilgrim children been naughty or nice?

It didn't matter, since the Pilgrims worked all through Christmas Day. The Pilgrims didn't believe in celebrating Christmas because they didn't think anyone could really know what day Jesus was born.

Guess why the Indians weren't around:

a) They heard the Pilgrims were coming so they took off in a hurry.

b) They were killed by a plague.

c) They were spending the winter in sunny Florida.

d) They weren't really gone; they were just hiding in the woods.

Unfortunately, the answer is letter *b*. A plague had wiped out all of the nearby Indians. The European sailors and fur traders, who had come to the New World before the Pilgrims, had carried diseases—probably smallpox and tuberculosis. The diseases were deadlier than any guns or cannons. In three years, they had wiped out an incredible three-fourths of the Indians who lived along the New England coast.

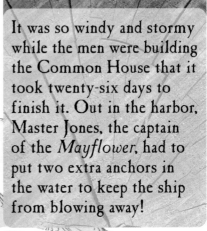

Sometimes the Pilgrims' settlement is called Plymouth Plantation. Even though you might think of a plantation as a big farm in the South where slaves worked before the Civil War, a *plantation* is also the name for a place to start a colony.

It was so windy and stormy while the men were building the Common House that it took twenty-six days to finish it. Out in the harbor, Master Jones, the captain of the *Mayflower*, had to put two extra anchors in the water to keep the ship from blowing away!

Did the Pilgrims build log cabins?

No, the first log cabins in America were built a little later by Swedish settlers in Delaware. The Pilgrims built frame houses just like the ones where they had lived in England, only smaller. The houses were built really close together, for safety, and they were all similar.

If you were a Pilgrim, you'd never lose your house key—because it was attached to the door! Pilgrims used wooden pegs attached to a string that pulled the latch to open a door.

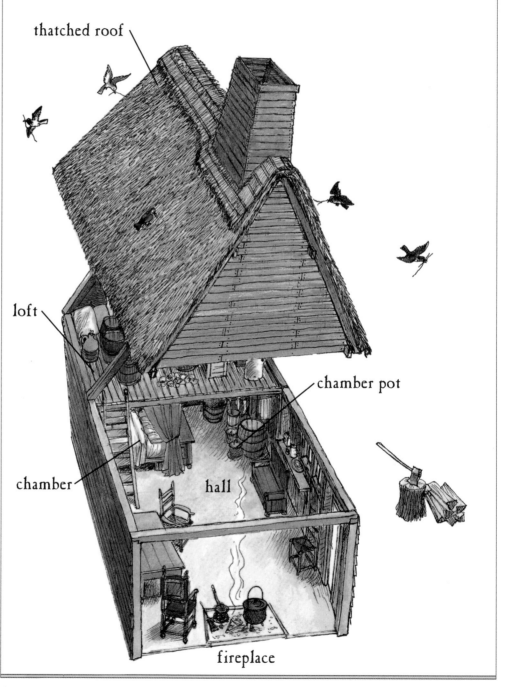

thatched roof

loft

chamber pot

chamber

hall

fireplace

Would everyone have his or her own bedroom?

Not by a long shot! Most of the first houses had only one room, but a few had two squarish rooms and a loft. Living in a house in Plymouth was only a little less crowded than living on the *Mayflower*.

The *hall* was the main room in the house. It had a huge fireplace. This is where Pilgrims cooked, ate, played, and worked.

The *chamber* was a small room in the back of the house for sleeping. Young children often slept in *trundle beds*, which slid underneath the parents' big bed during the day.

Food was stored in the *loft*. And the bathrooms? They weren't much better than they'd been on the *Mayflower*. The Pilgrims used *chamber pots*, which had to be emptied outside.

The small windows weren't made of glass, which was very expensive and much too fragile to carry across the ocean. Instead, windows were covered with oiled paper or wooden shutters. This made the houses very dark. At night, some light came from the fireplace or lamps or candles.

Thatched roofs were pretty sturdy, but they had to be repaired all the time because birds borrowed the thatch for their nests. And there was always the danger that the roof might catch fire with sparks from the chimney. (Or from Francis Billington's firecrackers!)

"Sleep tight, don't let the bedbugs bite!" The Pilgrims could have used this expression. In their day, mattresses were placed on the floor or held on to bed frames by ropes. After a while, the ropes would sag. "Sleep tight" means sleeping in a bed where the ropes are pulled tight. And "bedbugs"? Insects lived in the mattresses, which were stuffed with straw, corn husks, oak leaves, or cattails. The insects often bit people as they slept.

What was the Pilgrims' first winter like?

That first winter in Plymouth was pretty grim for the Pilgrims. Many of them got sick, and more than half of them died.

Some of the Pilgrims probably had *scurvy*, a disease people get when they don't eat enough foods that contain vitamin C. (There was no fresh fruit or vegetables aboard the *Mayflower*.) Some may have caught pneumonia, or typhus from the lice on the ship. And the cold, windy weather in Plymouth only made the sick people sicker.

Why did the Pilgrims bury their dead at night?

The settlers were afraid that Indians might attack if they knew how few Pilgrims were left. So it's said that they buried their dead in the dark and didn't mark the graves.

Did the Pilgrims have a doctor?

Well, kind of. Samuel Fuller, who came over on the *Mayflower*, was called a surgeon even though he probably didn't have any formal medical training. Mr. Fuller was a deacon in the church, a job that unofficially made him responsible for his congregation's health. Mr. Fuller did as much as he could to help the sick Pilgrims, but in the seventeenth century there were no medicines that could cure what the Pilgrims had.

When the Pilgrims suffered only minor aches and pains, they took medicine made of herbs the women planted in their gardens. If a Pilgrim was sicker than that, Mr. Fuller would bleed him. That meant he would—yikes!—cut open a vein in the patient's arm to let the sickness drain out, along with some blood. (This didn't work, but the Pilgrims didn't know any better.) As for surgery, the only kind the Pilgrims had was amputation—without any painkillers!

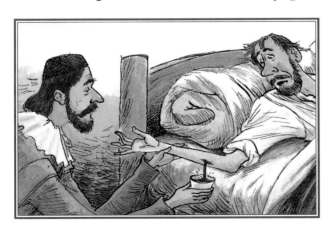

Pilgrims thought it was dangerous to wash their bodies. They believed that the worst infections came from the spirits in wind and water, so they rarely bathed. Can you imagine how bad they must have smelled? They may actually have used perfume, but, since everyone smelled the same way, it's likely that no one really knew the difference. Eeeuuw.

Were the Pilgrims scared of the Indians?

Probably. They'd heard lots of stories back in England and Holland. And their early encounters with the Indians hadn't been friendly. The first men to go exploring had been shot at with arrows.

It was three months before the Pilgrims met their Indian neighbors. Boy, were they in for a surprise!

What happened when the Pilgrims met their first Indian neighbor?

The Pilgrims certainly weren't expecting an Indian to stroll right into Plymouth. And they definitely weren't expecting to hear him speak English! But that's exactly what happened.

The Pilgrim kids were probably dying to tell their friends back home what real Indians looked like. The Indians wore lots of ornaments on their clothes and bodies. They decorated themselves with porcupine quills, beads, and paint and carried bows and arrows made of eagle claws and bear teeth. The Pilgrims' clothes looked pretty boring compared to the Indians'!

An Indian named Samoset, wearing only a leather belt with fringe in front, introduced himself to the Englishmen and asked for beer. The Pilgrims gave him what they had—*strong water* (a kind of liquor), biscuits, butter, cheese, pudding, and a piece of duck meat. They also lent him a long red coat to put on because the Pilgrims were embarrassed that he was almost naked.

Samoset told the Pilgrims he wanted to spend the night in Plymouth. The Pilgrims didn't want to offend their visitor, so they let him stay in one of the Pilgrims' houses. Before Samoset left, the Pilgrims gave him gifts of a knife, ring, and bracelet.

How did Samoset know English?

Samoset was an Algonkian Indian chief from what is now Maine. He had come to the area around Plymouth with an English explorer just a few months before the Pilgrims arrived. The English fishermen and explorers had taught Samoset

English. Now he had a job as an interpreter.

Samoset told the Pilgrims about the Patuxet Indians who had lived at Plymouth. He told how they had all died of a strange sickness that killed most of the New England Indians.

Who was Squanto?

Samoset came back a few days later with five hungry Indian friends. The Pilgrims fed the Indians, and in exchange for the food, the Indians danced and sang. The English had never seen anything like the Indians' performance.

One of the Indians who accompanied Samoset was named Tisquantum. The Pilgrims called him Squanto. He spoke even better English than his Algonkian friend. Why? Squanto had actually been to England! He had been kidnapped by an English captain who tried to sell him into slavery in Spain. But he had escaped to England, where a London merchant helped him get back home.

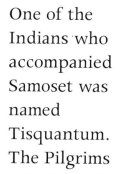

Squanto's tribe was the Patuxet, one of the Wampanoag tribes that had lived right where Plymouth now stood. When Squanto returned to his home, all he found were bones scattered across the fields. A plague had wiped out so many Indians that not even enough had survived to bury the dead. So lonely Squanto had gone to live with another nearby tribe of Wampanoags.

Squanto was the Pilgrims' greatest friend. He lived with them for the rest of his life. Without Squanto's help, the Pilgrims almost certainly would have died.

Why did the Pilgrims bury fish in the ground with their corn?

This was a farming secret Squanto taught them. The fish, called herring, acted as a fertilizer and made the corn grow better. Squanto showed the Pilgrims how to plant the corn kernels in little hills, with two or three fish in each. He said to plant the corn when the buds on the oak trees were "as big as a mouse's ear." Without the corn Squanto helped the Pilgrims plant (which was the corn they'd stolen when they first arrived), the colonists would have starved.

What did Squanto show the Pilgrims?

a) where the wild herbs grew

b) which wild berries and plants were safe for them to eat

c) where to catch fish and eels

d) how to hunt turkey, deer, and other animals with nets, hooks, spears, and even their bare hands

e) all of the above

The answer is e, all of the above.

Did the Pilgrims and the Indians get along?

Thanks to Squanto, they did. One of the greatest things Squanto did for the Pilgrims was to serve as a translator between the Indians and the Pilgrims. He helped the Pilgrims make an important peace treaty with the *sachem*, or leader, of the Wampanoags, Chief Massasoit.

Massasoit arrived on a hill near Plymouth with sixty men. Edward Winslow was sent to *parley*, or speak, with him. Squanto served as interpreter. Winslow agreed to stay on the hill as a hostage while Massasoit and twenty of his men went to talk with Governor Carver. Massasoit and the governor sat on cushions in an unfinished house, where they ate, drank, and agreed to be friends. The treaty was important to both groups, especially because the Indian tribes to the west might attack either the Wampanoags or the Pilgrims. The peace guaranteed by the treaty lasted for more than fifty years.

What did the treaty say?

- That the Pilgrims and the Wampanoags would never attack each other. If anyone did, he would be punished.

- If one group was attacked, the other would help defend it.

- The Indians and colonists would not carry weapons when visiting each other.

- No stealing was allowed.

- The Indians would return some tools they had taken from the Pilgrims.

The colonists were relieved that they would be safe. One of the Pilgrims, Edward Winslow, wrote that the Pilgrims could now walk "as peaceably and safely in the wood as in the highways in England."

Could Indians be *too* friendly?

After Massasoit and Governor Carver made the peace treaty, more and more Wampanoags came to visit Plymouth. And they were always hungry! If these visits continued, the Pilgrims were going to run out of food. Finally, the Pilgrims sent messengers to Massasoit to ask him, politely, to stop his people from visiting so often. He agreed.

Things between the English and the Indians went downhill years later, after William Bradford (the second governor of Plymouth Plantation) and Chief Massasoit died. The English got mad because the Indians were killing their cattle that were destroying the Indians' cornfields. The Indians got mad because the English were taking their land and imposing their religion.

In 1675 the Wampanoag attacked the English settlers. The battles that followed were called King Philip's War, because Philip is what the Europeans called Massasoit's son, the new Wampanoag leader. Both sides fought long and hard, but the Indians eventually lost the war.

The Pilgrim children practiced reading with a *horn book*, made of a cow's horn with a piece of paper printed with the ABCs attached to it. A thin sheet of see-through animal horn covered the paper to protect it.

Did children go to school in Plymouth?

No. Starting a colony was a lot of work. From the time they were four or five, children worked as part of the family team. The most important part of their education was learning how to make and do the things they needed to survive.

When the Pilgrim children weren't working, they learned to read at home. There weren't any children's books around, but there was the Bible.

What kind of chores did Pilgrim children do?

They didn't have to mow the lawn or load the dishwasher, but they did have all sorts of chores to keep them busy. Can you guess which list of chores belonged to boys, and which to girls?

- Cleaning the house, making beds, washing, cooking
- Growing herb gardens
- Caring for younger children

- Helping hunt, fish, and farm
- Making *trunnels* or *treenails* (the wooden pegs used to build houses)
- Watching the cornfields for dogs or wolves who might eat the crops and then throwing stones at any who came.

Some chores were done by both girls and boys. They made mattresses by stuffing straw, feathers, tufts of wool, cattails, or corn husks into linen bags. They weeded gardens, picked mussels, dug for clams, gathered reeds to use for thatching roofs, and collected kindling.

Do you have any friends named "Love" or "Remember"?

Some of the Pilgrims had unusual names! Even though most Pilgrims had common names like Sarah, Mary, or John, Pilgrim parents sometimes named their children after their own hopes and values. Among the *Mayflower* children were Love and Wrastling Brewster, Remember Allerton, Resolved White, Humility Cooper, and Desire Minter.

I'M RESOLVED

UM, RESOLVED TO WHAT?

The first Pilgrim baby born in the New World was named Peregrine. The name means "wanderer," so it's funny that Peregrine ended up doing the opposite. Instead of roaming, he stayed in New England until he was eighty-three, dying only ten miles from where he was born.

The Pilgrims didn't have silver buckles on their hats and shoes, the way we often see them drawn. Those buckles are something artists just made up over time.

TRUE or FALSE ## All the Pilgrims' clothes were black and white, and stiff.

False. The Pilgrims actually wore very colorful clothes, though the garments probably lost some of their brightness from all the wear and tear. We're not talking crazy polka dots and plaids, but the Pilgrims' everyday clothes were red-brown, blue, green, and purple.

So why do we always see pictures of Pilgrims in black hats and clothes with stiff white collars? Some Pilgrims did have these kinds of clothes, but they wore them only for their Sabbath, on Sundays.

Once they were about six years old, or *upgrown* (grown up), children dressed like miniature adults.

parents or siblings used *leading strings* (attached at the shoulders) to help the child learn to walk

puddings protected toddlers' heads in case they fell as they were learning to walk

long clothes (a long dress) were worn by both boys and girls until they were about six years old

34

white linen *coif* covered the ears

thick knitted *Monmouth cap*

waist coat was a fitted, long-sleeved jacket fastened in the front

wool or leather *doublet* (jacket that fastens in the front)

breeches came to the knees

long wool skirt

wool stockings

coat or cape in cold weather

Remember Francis Billington, who set off the fireworks on the *Mayflower*? His brother, John, was also a troublemaker. Young John wandered into the woods one day and got lost. His parents worried that he would starve or be captured by unfriendly Indians.

A few days later, the Pilgrims heard that John was with the nearby Nauset Indians. John was covered with feathers and "behung with beads." (He had many Indian necklaces around his neck.) The Pilgrim adults were angry because John had worried them, but the children were in awe of his new jewelry and the tales of his adventure.

If the Pilgrims were so religious, why didn't they build a church?

The Pilgrims worshiped in a building called a *meetinghouse* instead of a church because they believed the church was the people, not the building. The meetinghouse was just a regular building that was also used for town meetings and as the fort. Nothing in the building suggested that the Pilgrims' meetinghouse was a church. It was simple and spare. Even their wooden benches were bare.

What was a typical Sunday service like?

Looooong! Practically all of Sunday was spent at the meetinghouse, with one service lasting from eight A.M. until noon and another from two until five or six P.M. Religious services weren't exactly *fun*, but they were a welcome change of pace from daily work and physical labor.

How did the Pilgrims practice their religion on other days?

Religion was the most important part of the Pilgrims' lives. Before and after every meal and at the start and end of each day, the father or head of the household read aloud a chapter of the Bible and prayed. At the end of the workday, he listened to his children's ABCs and asked them questions about religion. Another Bible chapter and more prayers came before bedtime.

Pilgrim households were strict. Children were expected to do as they were told. Parents taught their children to fear God and respect their elders. If they did these things and obeyed God's commandments, they were told they could look forward to another life after death.

Guess which of the following were laws in Plymouth:

a) Everyone had to go to church on Sundays.

b) No stealing.

c) No getting drunk.

a) No malicious (harmful) statements about other people.

e) All of the above.

All of the above were laws made by the colony's elected leaders. Mostly the people of Plymouth obeyed and respected the laws. When they didn't, common punishments for committing minor crimes, like disobeying a parent or scolding your husband in public, included having your head and feet tied together or being whipped or fined.

It won't surprise you that John Billington, the father of troublemakers Francis and John, Jr., was arrested for refusing to take his turn guarding the colony. When he was sentenced to have his neck and heels tied together, he quickly changed his mind!

Ms. Manners would probably have had a fit seeing Pilgrims eat. Pilgrims used their hands to eat—unless they were having soup.

Each person had his or her own sharp knife to cut meat, cheese, bread, and butter. This was the same knife you'd use to cut wood!

Trenchers were plates made of wood with one flat side and one side hollowed out for soup. Children shared trenchers with their siblings.

Everyone shared one bowl for drinking, which might have had from four handles to none.

Dirty dishes were usually scraped and then washed in hot water without soap. Water for washing, cooking, and drinking had to be carried from the town brook, which ran just behind the Pilgrims' houses.

What were meals like in Plymouth?

The Pilgrims' food was bland, bland, bland. They didn't have many spices, and there was hardly anything sweet.

Pork was the main meat, but rabbits found in the woods and countryside were a favorite meal. The Pilgrims also ate boiled chickens, wild fowl, turkey, and venison.

Seafood was not the delicacy it is today. The Pilgrims ate it so often that just the sight of it probably made them, well, crabby.

Water was the main drink. Families also made their own beer every few weeks.

The Pilgrims ate many kinds of bread, which they baked in outdoor ovens that everyone shared. The bread had a different taste and texture than you're used to today—it was harder and grainier. But it was also more nutritious, made of wheat and rye flour and ground cornmeal. Corn bread was the most common type of bread in early Plymouth.

Would you like the Pilgrims' bread?

See for yourself! You probably don't have a big outdoor oven, but you can make this more modern version of the Pilgrims' bread in a griddle. Small, round *bannocks* similar to these were served at almost every meal.

Find an adult to help you follow this easy recipe. When you're done, don't forget to eat the cakes with your hands, like the Pilgrims did!

✨ INGREDIENTS ✨

1 cup water

1 cup stone-ground cornmeal

1/2 teaspoon salt

1/2 cup milk

1 egg

2 tablespoons butter

1) Ask an adult to bring the water to a boil.

2) In a bowl, mix the cornmeal and salt together. Have the adult add the boiling water, and stir the mixture with a spoon until smooth. Then stir in the milk. Let the batter sit for about five minutes. Then beat in the egg.

3) Have the adult melt the butter in a frying pan over medium heat. Then use a tablespoon to drop the batter onto the pan and cook the cakes until golden brown on one side (about two minutes). Have the adult turn the cakes with a spatula and cook the other side about a minute. Serve hot or cold!

If your mother asked thee to fetch a *pipkin* so she could make *forced eggs*, she wanted you to get a saucepan so she could make scrambled eggs. Here are some other Pilgrim words:

whortleberries—blueberries

pompions—pumpkins

hasty pudding—oatmeal or cornmeal cereal

victuals—food

pap—milk and flour mixed together; the first solid food Pilgrim babies ate

The Pilgrims' feast wasn't actually the first Thanksgiving in the New World. The Indians had been having similar harvest feasts for many years. Spanish settlers in the Southwest and English settlers in Virginia also had them, before the Pilgrims even arrived in America.

The Pilgrims called their harvest feast "Thanksgiving."

False. To the Pilgrims, a true thanksgiving was a day of fasting and prayer. And though they surely prayed before their meal, as they always did, the Pilgrims certainly didn't fast at their feast!

What we now call the first Thanksgiving was really more of a harvest festival. It was a chance for the Pilgrims to celebrate what they had achieved and share with their Indian friends who had helped to make it all possible.

Did the Pilgrims and Indians eat turkey, cranberry sauce, and pumpkin pie at the first Thanksgiving?

Yes and no. The Pilgrims served every kind of food they could get their hands on. From the forest there were ducks, geese, wild turkeys, wild onions to make a *sallet* (salad), and wild berries, including cranberries (but not cranberry sauce); from the waters there were cod, salmon, bass, eels, lobster, mussels, oysters, and clams; and from the Pilgrims' gardens there were pumpkins (but not pumpkin pie), carrots, cabbages, radishes, turnips, onions, beets, and *cowcumbers* (cucumbers). There were also cornmeal breads and puddings.

Can you guess what a "crane berry" is? The Pilgrims called the sour red berries the Indians showed them "crane berries" because they thought the plant's flowers looked like the nodding head of the water bird. The Pilgrims also called the berries "marsh whortleberries." Today we call them cranberries.

Who was at the Pilgrims' Thanksgiving?

Massasoit came to the feast, but the Pilgrims didn't know he was going to bring ninety Indians with him. There wasn't enough food for that many people. So Massasoit sent a few of his best hunters into the woods. They solved the problem by returning with five deer.

At the outdoor celebration, "trestle tables" were made of sawhorses with wooden planks laid across them. There were a few stools and tree stumps to sit on, but many people, including the Indians and probably the children, sat on the ground.

If there wasn't any football to watch on TV, what did everyone do during three days of Thanksgiving?

The first Thanksgiving, held in mid-October (not November), lasted for three whole days. When it got dark, everyone went to bed. In the morning they got up and started partying all over again!

The men and boys had running and jumping contests and played games. The Pilgrims shot muskets at targets, and the Indians shot with bows and arrows. The Pilgrims held a military parade. The Indians danced.

The women and girls spent most of the time cooking. Since only four women had survived the first winter, the children and servants had to help prepare the feast.

What happened after the Pilgrims' Thanksgiving party?

The early settlers at Plymouth had to make do with limited resources, especially food. More settlers arrived right after the Thanksgiving feast, and they came without supplies. That meant more mouths to feed and people to house.

Thanksgiving was not celebrated as an official holiday until 1777, when the Continental Congress declared it a national holiday, to celebrate the colonists' defeating the British at Saratoga during the American Revolution. The first presidents proclaimed national Thanksgivings, but by 1815 the custom had almost died out again. In 1837 writer Sarah Josepha Hale began a long campaign to reinstate the holiday.

In 1863 President Abraham Lincoln proclaimed the national holiday, to be celebrated the last Thursday in November. President Franklin D. Roosevelt moved the date to the third Thursday in November in 1939, but many Americans didn't like that. So in 1941, when Congress declared Thanksgiving a national holiday, Roosevelt compromised and proclaimed Thanksgiving the fourth Thursday in November. This is when we celebrate today.

But things got better as time went on. The Pilgrims had learned—with the help of the Indians—how to provide for themselves. Their families were healthy. They could worship as they chose. And relations with the Indians were good. By the late 1620s the colony was thriving, and the Pilgrims were able to bring over many of the family members and friends they had left behind.

Today about one in every six Americans has a relative who came over on the *Mayflower*. Famous descendants of *Mayflower* Pilgrims include Presidents John Adams and John Quincy Adams, Zachary Taylor, Ulysses S. Grant, James Garfield, Franklin D. Roosevelt, George Bush, and George W. Bush.

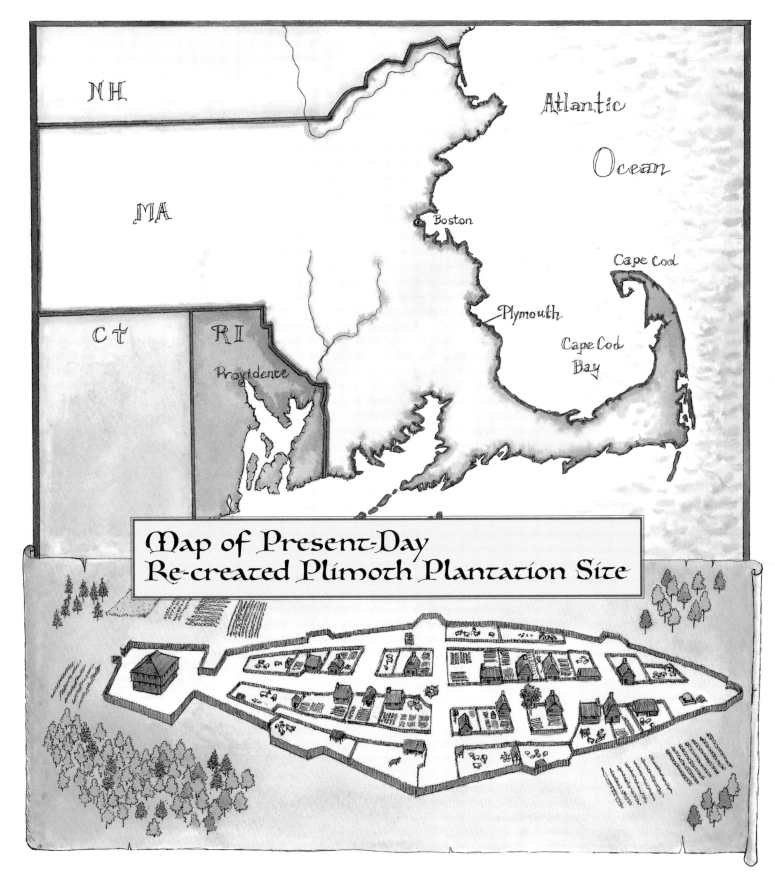

NH

Atlantic

Ocean

MA

Boston

Cape Cod

Plymouth

Cape Cod
Bay

CT

RI

Providence

Map of Present-Day
Re-created Plimoth Plantation Site

Mayflower II

PLIMOTH PLANTATION
PLYMOUTH, MASSACHUSETTS